THE HEYDAY OF THE LONDON BUS-2

Kevin McCormack

IAN ALLAN
Publishing

First published 1995

ISBN 0 7110 2344 1

© Kevin McCormack 1995

Published by Ian Allan Publishing

an imprint of Ian Allan Ltd, Terminal House, Station Approach, Shepperton, Surrey TW17 8AS.
Printed by Ian Allan Printing Ltd, Coombelands House, Coombelands Lane, Addlestone, Weybridge, Surrey KT15 1HY.

Front Cover:
What a Scorcher!
The passengers have taken full advantage of the RT's generous window apertures on this hot summer's day in July 1973. RT3395 passes St Patrick's church in Griffin Road, Plumstead. *Dave Edwards*

Back cover:
Springtime in Abinger Hammer
It's a case of Green Line turning to Yellow Line for demoted RF219, seen here on 14 April 1972 calling at one of several attractive Surrey villages on the A25 between Guildford and Dorking. *R. C. Riley*

Title page:
Royal Visitor
Well-groomed RT1009 climbs the hill towards Windsor Castle during the summer of 1976 on a short working of route 441. After turning at the Bells of Ouzeley, the bus headed for the village of Hedgerley which boasted a delightful old hostelry where the author spent many 'happy' hours during his youth.

Introduction

Environmentally Friendly
There is an abundance of green in this July 1973 shot of Green Line coach RF43 outside Juniper Hall, Mickleham, the venue for many a school geography field trip. This 22-year-old vehicle has a long run ahead of it on route 713 to St Albans via Victoria. This service ceased to operate in January 1977. *Dave Edwards*

Published three years ago, *The Heyday of London's Buses* proved to be remarkably successful and, therefore, we are pleased to be able to bring you another selection of colour illustrations from the great days of London's buses.

The traditional London bus continues to be a source of fascination, not just to today's tourists hopping on Routemasters in central London but also to the large body of enthusiasts and ordinary travellers who recall with vivid affection the buses which were so familiar throughout London, its suburbs and surrounding countryside: memories of a more ordered world in which little seemed to change — when London Transport (LT) buses could be found anywhere within a 25-mile radius of Charing Cross. This was an area covering nearly 2,000 square miles and stretching from Baldock to Horsham, Guildford to Ongar and Aylesbury to Tonbridge.

Times, of course, have changed and the process continues unabated. London Country, which assumed control of the Green (Country Area) buses and coaches in 1970, has been split up and sold off. Now it's the turn of London Transport. Already, competitive tendering for certain routes has seen the erosion of the red bus monopoly and even some of London's celebrated Routemasters have changed colour. The bus wheels are turning full circle to the pre-1933 days before LT was formed, when there was a proliferation of transport companies trying to win passengers. Luckily, the authorities have now realised that an important part of London's heritage — its red buses — might vanish.

Consequently, the new operators will have to paint their vehicles red. Add to this the fact that 500 Routemasters have been refurbished for at least another 10 years' service and we have some chance of retaining one famous tradition for the foreseeable future.

Now back to the book and to the period up to 1979, that watershed year which marked the demise of the standard postwar double and single-deckers — the RT and RF respectively. How time marches on! It's sad to think that anyone under 20 won't even remember these buses in normal service. I make no apologies for featuring so many buses of the RT family in this album. After all, there were almost 7,000 built, they were virtually unseen outside LT's operating area and they are firm favourites amongst enthusiasts. However, the RT's contemporaries have not been forgotten, nor have some of the types which ran alongside the RT towards the end and even at the start of the type's long and distinguished career. Colour photographs from the late 1940s are very rare and it is a treat to be able to include some here.

The preservation movement continues to grow, helping to keep memories and interest alive. It is reputed that one-seventh of the RF fleet is preserved — that's an amazing 100 buses! More recently, a new phenomenon has emerged: heritage services using 'vintage' vehicles. Only today, as I start on this introduction, my local paper reports on the forthcoming exploits of Leatherhead garage's recently-acquired Routemaster and Guildford garage is busily preparing GS13 for another summer Sunday season around the Surrey hills, where it will meet up with RF136. I have no doubt that this market will develop over the years to come.

Now for some credits. This book would not have materialised without the help of

Suburban Survivor

Right: For those living in the London suburbs in the 1950s, 1960s and, for some, even the 1970s the red RT-type was the familiar local bus. Typical of these is RT1627, on the Bromley-Lewisham service 94, which is seen at Southborough on 10 November 1974, nearly four years before this service lost its RTs. *Author's Collection*

Upstairs, Downstairs

Below: From 1953 until 1967, British European Airways owned a fleet of 65 one-and-a-half-deck coaches. They were so designed that the passengers sitting in the rear half of the vehicle sat on their cases or, more precisely, on a raised section above the luggage compartment. The vehicles, which were operated on BEA's behalf by LT, were withdrawn in 1966 and 1967, apart from one example, and many, like these in this July 1970 view at Richmond, saw further use. MLL720 had a particularly interesting second life after withdrawal by BEA, as it visited many of the continental towns and cities that had been displayed on its flight destination indicators.

other photographers, since much of my material saw the light of day in the first collection. I am particularly grateful to David Thrower of RT2794/RTL1050 fame for introducing me to Dave Edwards and Jim Collins. They provided much of the 1970s material. Thanks are also due to Mr C. Carter for his remarkable early transparencies, to Steve Fennell and to those eminent railway photographers, Dick Riley and Geoff Rixon, for their contributions. Finally, thanks are due to Bill Ballard and Julian Bowden for their assistance. All the uncredited photographs are the author's work.

I hope that you will enjoy this second bus ride into the past. Hold tight and have your fares ready please!

Kevin R. McCormack
Ashtead,
Surrey,
May 1994

Bridging the Gap
Southend comes to south London as a hired Leyland PD3 passes under the railway bridge in Marlpit Lane, Coulsdon, on 6 January 1976. Vehicle shortages caused LT to borrow 10 of these buses from Southend Corporation to operate out of Croydon garage on route No 190 between September 1975 and February 1976. The buses were then passed on to London Country, which had similar vehicle problems, for use at Harlow. *Jim Collins*

Making a Splash
An unidentified RT-type displays its amphibious abilities at Blackheath. It was noticeable that the RTs and Routemasters were prepared to rush through the floods, whilst the newer DMSs crawled through more gingerly. *Jim Collins*

Last Orders

Above: The Royal Forest Hotel, on the edge of Epping Forest, was a popular watering hole for intending passengers right up to 1968, when a new terminus was built at Chingford station. In this 1949 view, Massey-bodied Guy Arab G176, built in 1945 to a wartime austerity design, is flanked by two STs, which dated from 1929/31 and whose days are numbered. The square cab of green ST1128, working red route No 38 to Victoria, reveals its origins to be an ex-East Surrey vehicle. RTs replaced STs on route No 38 in September 1949 and RTWs took over the 145 in February 1950. *C. Carter*

Old Standard

Right: With 2,701 members, the STL-type (which represented a lengthened ST-type) became LT's first standard bus. It originated in 1932 following government approval of longer and heavier twin-axled double-deck buses. Crawley-based STL2263 started life as a red bus at Palmers Green but is wearing pre-1946 Country Area green (with black mudguards instead of green) in this shot taken at Purley. *C. Carter*

Beauty and the Beast

Left: In November 1974, London Country hired 12 Daimler Fleetlines from Bournemouth Corporation and put them to work at Leatherhead garage for route No 408. Short on good looks, Bournemouth No 197 is passed at West Croydon by battered RT1018. The appearance of the latter was transformed in 1977 when it was one of only four RTs selected for overhaul and repainting. Subsequently a driver training vehicle, RT1018 became London Country's very last active RT. *Dave Edwards*

Driving Ambition

Below left: A new recruit takes to the streets whilst his instructor poses for the camera. TD54, seen here leaving Fulwell trolleybus depot in 1962, had been withdrawn from passenger service following replacement of a weak bridge at Walton-on-Thames. Dating from only 1945, this Leyland Tiger with Mann Egerton bodywork looks distinctly antiquated considering that London Transport's predecessor, the LGOC, had full-fronted single-deckers with side-mounted engines as early as 1932. But with no single-deckers obtained during the war, and a need for new vehicles when hostilities ended, LT had to take what was available from AEC and Leyland. As a result it purchased 131 TDs and 80 similar-looking Ts. The TDs were the last Central Area (red) buses to have crash gearboxes and, since they were relatively young when withdrawn, many found further passenger use, including several which were sold to Ceylon (Sri Lanka). *Geoff Rixon*

Green Field Sight

Right: RT2344 takes the scenic route from Woolwich Arsenal to Croydon as it crosses Blackheath on 15 November 1976. *Jim Collins*

Surprise Bullseye

Above: Over six months of London Country ownership has elapsed and RF175 has so far managed to retain its London Transport appearance. Seen here at Heathrow Airport, this RF was one of 175 modernised in the mid-1960s to extend their lives for service on Green Line coach routes.

What's the Bottom Line?

Right: It's a case of destination unknown for RT2631 at West Norwood station on 23 July 1975, an omen perhaps of its replacement by one-person operated buses two weeks later. *Author's Collection*

Out of Retirement

Left: The first London trolleybus returns to its old stamping ground at Hampton in April 1962 for a test run in preparation for a commemorative journey to mark the last day of trolleybus operation on 8 May. This ancient contraption, one of a class of 60 nicknamed 'Diddlers', entered service in 1931 and ran until 1949. It was then stored out of the public eye at Reigate garage along with other historic vehicles now on display in the London Transport Museum at Covent Garden (or in the reserve collection). Imagine my incredulity when, as an uninformed schoolboy visiting Fulwell depot in April 1962, I opened a mysterious door and discovered No 1 being serviced. It looked distinctly jaded and I thought at first that it was a tram.
Geoff Rixon

Twilight Years

Right: The 151-strong prewar RT-type, built between 1939 and 1942, is represented here by RT128 at Fulwell trolleybus depot eking out its final days as a trainer. This example was one of seven which enjoyed an extra two years of passenger service until 1957 due to a weak bridge on the No 327 route at Broxbourne in Hertfordshire. Until it was strengthened this bridge was barred to the heavier postwar RTs. Ironically, the prewar RTs replaced more modern STLs on this service; the latter were non-standard but had a worthwhile resale value.
Geoff Rixon

Village Transport

Left: This enormous 72-seater Leyland Atlantean is unlikely to find many passengers in Mickleham, near Boxhill in Surrey. AN37, pictured at The Running Horses in July 1973, belonged to a batch of 90 vehicles built in 1971/72. Introduced initially to replace the RTs, the class clocked up nearly 18 years of service. *Dave Edwards*

Antipodean Traveller

Above: The only non-standard double-deckers to remain after the completion of the standardisation programme in 1955 were the 76 members of the 'Regent Low Height' (RLH) class dating from 1950-52. RLH45 is seen here at Addlestone garage where several were required for route No 436 because of a low bridge outside Staines. The introduction of large-capacity single-deckers rendered the RLHs surplus to requirements by 1970 and after some changes of ownership RLH45 emigrated to New Zealand in November 1972. *Julian Bowden Collection*

Light Green Line

Above: The fourth of the prototype Routemasters and the only one to remain in service is pictured here at East Molesey. Starting life as 'Coach Routemaster Leyland' (CRL) 4 in October 1957, it was renumbered RMC4 in August 1961 after the suffix 'L' had come to signify 'Long' — whereas CRL4 was short! The vehicle received a front-end rebuild in December 1964 to match the production RMCs but was still distinguishable by its three-piece destination display and non-opening front windows. Between October 1960 and November 1962, RMC4 carried an experimental lighter shade of green, as shown here. *Geoff Rixon*

Grey Day

Right: With interior lights aglow, RT701 proceeds through Wallington in March 1972 on a service which replaced the No 654 trolleybus service. *Dave Edwards*

Heavy Metal

The 'Daimler Mono Standec' (DMS) was the ungainly new standard bus which was supposed to rid London of its RTs and RMs. However, largely due to its heavy weight, which put extra stress on the components, these vehicles tended to be unreliable and, indeed, the first members of the class were withdrawn simultaneously with the last RTs. Nevertheless, the class did achieve 22 years of operation, which was no mean feat, and many are still giving good service to other operators in less arduous conditions, such as on London sightseeing work. The RFs, on the other hand, thrived on tough conditions and in this scene at West Croydon on 15 May 1976 RF180 looks in fine fettle in its 25th year of Green Line coach operation. *Jim Collins*

Up the Wall

A convenient vantage point provides an insight into RT4529 as it stands in Belmont Road, Wallington, in February 1972. London Country inherited 484 RTs on its formation in 1970, representing nearly 70% of its double-deck fleet. With conductor operation uneconomic in the Country Area, the company resolved to dispose of RTs at the earliest opportunity and by the end of 1972 less than 100 remained in passenger service. Nevertheless, the No 403 route was to retain three of the last four survivors through to 1977, with the last (RT604) soldiering on until the summer of 1978. *Dave Edwards*

Brief Encounter

Left: It was certainly more by luck than judgement that RFs 522 and 471 were caught passing at Littleworth Common, near Esher, in January 1979. Observant readers familiar with the first *Heyday of London's Buses* will note that the Morris Minor has served before on RF patrol. Route No 219, together with the No 218, were the last red bus services operated by RFs which, like the RTs on the No 62, had enjoyed an unintended stay of execution. For the RFs the reason was because the larger replacement Leyland Nationals could not be accommodated in Kingston garage and an allocation exchange was necessary with nearby Norbiton garage, which took time to effect. The RFs' last day of service was 30 March 1979, eight days before the withdrawal of the surviving RTs.

Nice Guy

Above: Abbey Wood garage has clearly taken good care of its staff bus, which sits amongst the RTs in December 1971. The 84-strong GS class of Guy Vixens were LT's smallest buses after they had replaced the Leyland Cubs in 1953 and until the new generation of mini and midibuses appeared in the 1970s and 1980s. The GSs were intended for lightly-used and narrow routes in the Country Area but, during the 1960s, their sphere of operation diminished and they started to be sold off. LT retained a few into the 1970s, but not for public use. *R. C. Riley*

On the Boil

Left: The driver's thumbs-up sign may be a little premature because RT4526 is showing early signs of overheating as it stands in a traffic jam near Shooters Hill on a hot day in July 1973. *Dave Edwards*

Atlantean Express

Right: In 1965, LT purchased 50 new Leyland Atlanteans (designated XAs) and eight Daimler Fleetlines (XFs), which were the forerunners of a new generation of front-entrance, rear-engined double-deckers. Comparative tests were run between the XAs, XFs, RMLs and FRM1 (the prototype rear-engined Routemaster). The XFs passed to London Country in 1970 together with three XAs, which were exchanged for RMLs. Following the removal of restrictions on one-person operated double-deckers in 1967, the XAs and XFs were able to operate as intended, and XA50 moved to Croydon where it is seen in June 1972. New Daimler Fleetlines (DMSs), of very different appearance to the XFs, replaced the XAs and all 50, including the London Country trio, were sold in 1973 to Hong Kong, where they worked until 1980. Yet again, they were replaced by DMSs, acquired from LT, the final irony being that the latter were reclassified as XFs! *Dave Edwards*

Bad Vibes

Left: Popular with enthusiasts, but generally disliked by LT staff because it was noisy and heavy to drive, the Leyland version of the RT, the RTL, was still a successful vehicle, despite being eclipsed by the RT. The bodies were generally the same, LT having turned to Leyland for the chassis and engine because AEC, with whom it had an agreement for the supply of at least three-quarters of its new vehicle requirements, was unable to provide sufficient buses quickly enough. So it was that Leyland built 1,631 RTLs, roughly a third of the number of RTs. However, as a result of a downturn in passenger demand from the mid-1950s, which caused the premature withdrawal of earlier examples and the storage of some new ones until 1958, the whole class was never in service together. The supremacy of the RT is evidenced by the fact that when the last RTL was withdrawn from passenger service in November 1968, there were still over 3,000 RTs in operation. In this photograph, RTL1015 is seen in the Edgware Road. *Geoff Rixon*

Scout Movement

Above right: It's off to camp for the scouts of Reigate Grammar School in their school bus, former green RLH35. These Regent low-deckers achieved a saving in height of one foot through having long bench seats upstairs and a sunken offside gangway. This was a surprise photograph; I was waiting to capture an approaching RT on the 408 when the RLH appeared from nowhere.

Camera Shy

Right: The passengers on RF65 are giving the photographer the cold shoulder as their steed negotiates the Marble Arch island at the northeast corner of Hyde Park. The vehicle is in the traditional Green Line livery of the 1951-65 period, with pale green relief instead of the normal Country Area cream. It is, however, missing its wooden roofboards, as carried by the RF in the background. When this shot was taken in August 1965, RF65 had been working Green Line services for 14 years and it was shortly after this date that a programme was begun to update the appearance and comfort of 175 members of the class. It is a remarkable tribute to the RF's design and engineering that the last survivors could still be found on Green Line work right up to 1979. *Geoff Rixon*

Flat Out

Left: RT489 makes its Sunday afternoon detour down the M4 airport spur in June 1978. It was nothing short of amazing to see a 30-year-old bus on a normal stopping service taking unsuspecting passengers for a burn-up along the motorway. In case readers are wondering how I took the photograph and lived to write this book, I should explain that I was leaning out of the sunshine roof of an elderly Fiat 500 which was having some difficulty keeping ahead of the RT.

Shopping Trolley

Right: Kingston-upon-Thames on a busy Saturday afternoon as trolleybus No 1390 travels through the shopping centre, leaving RF466 behind at the lights. Trolleybus operation in Kingston was about to end after 31 years, resulting in the withdrawal of the last members of what was once the largest trolleybus fleet in the world, with, at one time, over 1,800 vehicles. London was a late convert to trolleybuses, introducing them on the back of the withdrawal of the trams in order to reuse as much as possible of the electrical plant and equipment. A trolleybus replacement programme was planned for 1959-62 using new Routemasters, although delays in their delivery meant that smaller RTs were used for the first three conversion stages. It was originally intended to operate the routes served by Fulwell and Isleworth depots through to the 1970s by retaining the newer vehicles built in 1948 and 1952, but an offer for both batches from Spain could not be resisted. So it was that the postwar trolleybuses were exported and older vehicles, like No 1390 (dating from 1939), were drafted in during 1961 and operated until the last day — 8 May 1962. But, arguably, the end of the London trolleybus really occurred, not at Kingston, but at La Coruña on 4 January 1979 when No 1815 was withdrawn from service.
Geoff Rixon

Big Brother

Left: Apart from the BEA Routemasters which were subject to length restrictions because of their towed trailers, all Routemasters built after 1964 were of the extended variety. This included all the Country Area vehicles such as RML2331, seen here at South Croydon on route 409. This service started life in 1922 as East Surrey's route S9, running from West Croydon to Uckfield, a phenomenal distance of 32 miles. Renumbered 409 in 1924, the route was cut back to Forest Row on LT's formation in 1933 although this destination was still outside the designated London area. *Dave Edwards*

All the Sixes

Right: Twenty-five years on and bovver boots are still with us, but RF666 has long since departed the scene. The RF is wearing early London Country livery, which was basically LT livery with the bullseye radiator cap cover painted over. The rear wheel discs were removed in 1972. *Author's Collection*

Missing Digit

Above: What purports to be brand new RT023 stands proudly outside Epping garage in early postwar livery while the ladies' escort studies the 1930s-style information display. Epping garage was closed in May 1963 when a replacement was opened at Harlow to cope with the expanding new town. *C. Carter*

City Worker

Right: RTL189, an early example of the RT's Leyland cousin, is about to be passed by two trolleybuses at Finsbury Square. Like RT1023 opposite, the RTL is new and wears early postwar livery, with partly-masked indicator panels for the reduced displays introduced as a wartime measure to save linen. *C. Carter*

31

Blinded by the Light

Left: A low winter sun creates glare for the driver of RT3607 as it passes through Farnham Royal in early 1977. By this time there were less than 20 operational RTs with London Country, but this example looks remarkably respectable considering it is still in the old livery with cream central relief band. RTs were officially replaced by Routemasters on the High Wycombe-Staines service in October 1972 but, as seen here, the RTs continued to appear for several years more.

Buses on Parade

Right: A line-up of six RTs dries off in the sunshine at Harrow Weald garage in early 1978. The five carrying blinds — RT4109, 3628, 4087, 4403 and, nearest the camera, 3232 — form part of the allocation of 28 required to operate the long 140 route from Mill Hill to Heathrow. RT3232, which had recently moved from Kingston following conversion of route 71, is interesting because it was one of the last survivors of the 34 RTs sold back by London Country to LT in September 1972. The only clue to their brief period away from home were the 'WILFUL DAMAGE TO SEATS' notices inside the saloons. Route 140 was the fourth last RT-operated LT service and for five glorious years I could watch the RTs from the comfort of my living room as they passed up and down High Street, Harlington. When I moved away to Surrey early in July 1978 I had no idea that the RTs were being replaced the following week, since the changeover date was not widely publicised.

Aerial View

Above: My former workplace at Heathrow Airport dominates this June 1968 photograph taken from the staff multi-storey car park. But the real interest lies in the vehicles in between, which include eight Routemasters, an RT, a Green Line RF, BEA's last 1½-deck coach (MLL740) and, in front of it, one of the shortlived AEC Reliance Executive Express coaches. Five of the Routemasters belong to

BEA; 65 of this type replaced the same number of 1½-deck coaches on the London-Heathrow service and were a familiar sight thundering down the M4 with their luggage trailers in tow. After this service ceased, the RMAs, as they were classified, eventually ended up with several different operators and one, still fitted with its towing hook, is regularly parked near my current workplace at Charing Cross for sightseeing duties.

Message from Mars

Right: Recently-repainted RT4610 turns out of Oxford Street in September 1974 on what was to become the last RT-operated route into central London. Notice the unusual interplanetary device fitted to the roof!

Fond Farewell

Left: Route 94 was the third last RT-operated service and Bromley garage has suitably decorated RT2146 for the final day on 25 August 1978. *Steve Fennell*

Mourning After

Above: It's the first day without RTs on route 247; brand-new Bristol single-decker BL11 stands at the Robin Hood & Little John, Brentwood, on 24 April 1976. *Bill Ballard Collection*

Variety Show

Left: Four different vehicle types are on offer at Kingston station on a site now occupied by an underpass. DMS606 is an example of the 'Londoner' class of Daimler Fleetlines introduced as a replacement for the RT and RM types but which ended up displacing the unfortunate AEC Merlin and Swift single-deckers such as SMS372 on the right. London Country had similar problems with its Swifts, represented here by SM104. These vehicles were unreliable from the start and did not present a fitting finale to the 60-year relationship between AEC and London's principal bus operators. RT2157, on the other hand, is a reminder of the manufacturer's illustrious past. Indeed, this vehicle went on to become a property: not exactly a 'des res' though, but an estate agent's office in Camden Town. *Dave Edwards*

Stop Gap

Below left: To help overcome London Country's acute vehicle shortage in the mid-1970s, various buses of untypical appearance were bought or hired. Three Leyland PD3/5s of 1961 vintage were purchased from Southdown Motor Services, designated LS1-3 and posted to Godstone garage for use on routes 409 and 411. LS1, in Southdown livery, stands at West Croydon in 1975. *Dave Edwards*

Number's Up

Right: Two weeks before its Certificate of Fitness expires, former Green Line coach RMC1504, with raised numberplate, passes through Whyteleafe on 29 November 1979. The last London Country Routemasters ran in normal service in February 1980, whereupon all the survivors were repurchased by LT. *Jim Collins*

No Sense of Direction
Passengers for West Molesey are in for a disappointment as RT2062 heads in the opposite direction and follows a trolleybus on to Kingston Bridge. New lamp standards are already in place in preparation for the removal of the poles and wires following the cessation of services four days later. The Boat Shop at Hampton Wick certainly enjoys a less cluttered view today. Notice that the RT still carries the offside route number, a practice which ceased in August 1963, and also blinds with upper-case lettering, a style which was gradually phased out from 1961. *Geoff Rixon*

Transatlantic Connections
London Bridge went to America and so did the RT seen crossing the replacement bridge on 20 June 1974 in the company of the local rag and bone man. RT2776 undertook an 8,000-mile goodwill tour between March and August 1952 and, since it was to give joy-rides, it was fitted with ventilation grilles in the roof for the benefit of a public more accustomed to air conditioning. When overhauled in January 1969, the body of RT2776 was fitted to RT1708 as part of the normal exchange process and the vehicle was withdrawn later in 1974. *R. C. Riley*

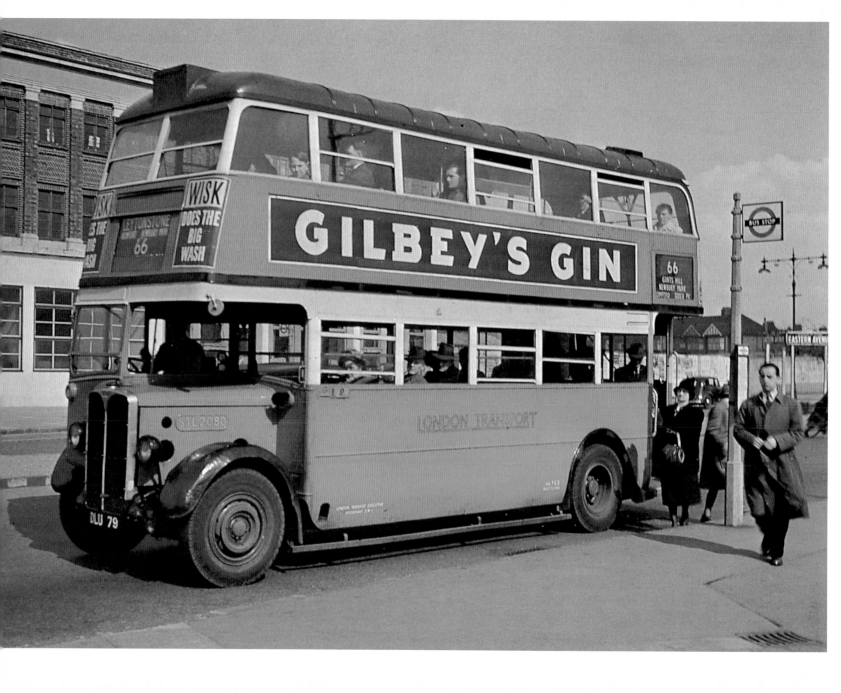

Body Changes

Left: STL2080, built in 1937 and seen here at Gants Hill in 1949, has just discarded its corroded Park Royal all-metal body in favour of a 1939 Chiswick-built product which had itself been displaced by a new RT body when the hybrid SRT-type was created. *C. Carter*

Portly Appearance

Above: With the move towards wider vehicles, LT ordered 500 Leyland eight-footers in 1948. Initially, they were restricted to suburban routes, but were eventually allowed to operate in central London, where they were most needed, in 1951. Classified RTW, these vehicles were rather noisy and heavy to drive like the narrower RTLs, and were the first members of the RT family to be replaced by the 8ft wide Routemasters after the latter had seen off the trolleybuses in 1962. The last RTW ran in passenger service in May 1966 and in the previous summer RTW190 is seen at Marble Arch. *Geoff Rixon*

Open and Shut Case

Above: RF441 reveals the driver's unusual vertical sliding window which was a feature of the RF class. As I was once to discover when driving an RF on private hire, this window could be very useful for pushing school girls through in order to open the air-operated doors manually from the inside after the girls had been playing with the doors and locked everyone out! RF441 was one of the 25 red survivors recertified for use on routes 218/219 between 1977 and March 1979. It acquired a white bullseye in the process. *Author's Collection*

Electrical Terminal

Right: A brand-new bus stop replacing the previous one attached to the green pole heralds the imminent demise of London's trolleybuses. No 1497 displays its rear end at The Dittons terminus of route 602. The trolleybus emblem on the window originated in 1935 and escaped the postwar redesign programme. *Geoff Rixon*

Passing the Time

Left: In the shadow of the clock tower, RT3520 takes a rest at Ongar on 23 July 1974 before returning to Harlow. The blue Southend-on-Sea Leylands previously borrowed by LT (see p4) ousted the RTs from the Harlow routes in March 1976. *Jim Collins*

Derby Runner

Right: The annual 406F service from Epsom station to the racecourse could normally be relied upon to produce some interesting vehicles as LT, and subsequently London Country, searched the darkest corners of their garages to find anything that could turn a wheel. On this occasion, East Grinstead garage has offered XF1 which is seen in Ashley Road on Derby Day. This bus was the first of a batch of six Daimler Fleetlines originally bought by LT in 1965 and used for comparative trials with the XAs and RMLs. Unlike the XAs which went to Hong Kong, the XFs stayed at home and the last survivor, XF3, clocked up a creditable 16 years of service. *Steve Fennell*

Misplaced Reliance

Below right: Another fickle product of the 1970s was the RP class of 90 AEC Reliance coaches, which were ordered by London Country to replace the crewed Coach Routemasters on Green Line services (or, in the case of route 727, to replace the RFs). The RPs started to enter service in December 1971; this view of RP6 at Rickmansworth predates 31 March 1972 because GS42 features in the background, behind the RF, on the last GS-operated service (the 336A to Loudwater village) which ceased on that date. Although some RPs continued on bus work until early 1984, sales and scrapping began in 1979 after only seven years' service. *Steve Fennell*

Right On Course

Left: It's back to Epsom again, but this time up on the Downs. RT4767, which has just crossed the five-furlong sprint track on its journey from Kingston, lurches into Great Tattenhams. No one is left in any doubt as to the RT's route number or destination, although how it intends to reach Redhill is anyone's guess. The 406 was officially converted to Routemaster operation on 24 February 1973, but Leatherhead and Reigate garages continued to dig up RTs from time to time with one lasting until early 1978.

Disowned

Above: What could easily be mistaken for the Wayside Manor's courtesy bus is in fact London Country's RF655 with an ill-placed advertisement over the fleet name. The RF is joined at Leatherhead garage by RT4480 in the days when red buses penetrated this part of Surrey. In fact, all the buses at Leatherhead up to 1933 were red, but this was because the garage belonged to the East Surrey Traction Co, which adopted this colour after starting off with blue. East Surrey was the operating agent for LGOC in this area and became a subsidiary of the latter in

1929. When the company acquired routes to the north of London in 1932 its name seemed inappropriate and was changed to London General Country Services. The following year, just before the company and its parent were swallowed up into London Transport, the red livery gave way to light and dark green, and green was subsequently maintained throughout LT's and London Country's tenure. This corner of east Surrey still boasts green buses because it is the colour adopted by the current occupiers of Leatherhead garage — London & Country.

Browned Off

Left: When bus building was allowed to resume during World War 2, the need for economy dictated Utility or austerity designs. A total of 435 Guy Arab double-deckers were purchased by LT during this period and G380, seen here at Romford in 1949, was one of the Weymann-bodied batch, built in the autumn of 1945 after

hostilities had ceased. A shortage of red paint meant that most Guys arrived from the manufacturers in various shades of brown and, like G380, they retained this shabby livery for some years. The Guys were displaced from route 103 in May 1952 and the whole class was withdrawn by the end of that year. Many were subsequently sold for service with provincial operators. *C. Carter*

Veteran Duo

Above: The LGOC introduced two standard double-deck classes in 1929 — the short-type (ST) 49-seat AEC Regent and the long-type (LT) three-axled, 60-seat AEC Renown. These were revolutionary buses for their time and served Londoners for some 20 years. In 1949 ST483 and LT473 stand in Kent Avenue, Dagenham. *C. Carter*

Factory Tour

Left: There's no shortage of passengers wishing to experience the delights of the Stevenage Industrial Area on 6 September 1971 as RT3247 prepares to leave the town centre. The bus has fared better than the shelter in managing to retain the bullseye emblem of its previous owner, but the driver's starched white summer coat and cap from a more dignified era have given way to shirtsleeves and braces. *R. C. Riley*

Not so Swift

Right: SMA12 was one of 21 AEC Swift coaches originally ordered by South Wales Transport but delivered instead to London Country in 1972 after being fitted-out for Green Line use. Although their enormous windows endeared them to passengers, they were somewhat under-powered for coach services and were eventually relegated to bus work before being withdrawn after less than 10 years' service. *Bill Ballard Collection*

Off-Colour

Below right: Here we have a pale-green RF coach, in a shade not dissimilar to the National Bus Company's leaf-green, working a red route. Sixteen RFs, plus CRL4/RMC4, were painted in this livery in 1960 in an attempt to brighten up the image of Green Line coaches but LT then had second thoughts and decided to stick with the darker Lincoln-green. A somewhat anaemic RF33, operating from Fulwell's former trolleybus depot, stands alongside Hampton Court station in March 1963 on a Sunday working of route 206 to Claygate. *Geoff Rixon*

Lazy Sunday

Above: The crew of RT625 find time to chat at Woolwich in October 1973 as RT4384 sets off for Crystal Palace. *Dave Edwards*

Competitive Edge

Right: Well-laden RT1536 out-accelerates an empty and younger AEC coach in the Edgware Road in May 1962. The RT is a Saunders-bodied example, ordered before the decision was taken to abandon roof number boxes. Because the bodies were non-standard, LT phased out these vehicles by 1971 in favour of the Park Royal and Weymann versions. *Geoff Rixon*

What a Shower!

Above: Inclement weather hits the village of Shere on 2 July 1972 as the flowerpot men seek shelter in RF251. *Dave Edwards*

Ringing the Changes

Right: All-over advertising became popular in the early 1970s and several Routemasters appeared in striking colours. Mobile telephone directory RM971 approaches St Paul's on 3 October 1972. *R. C. Riley*

Evening Shadows

Left: The poplars tremble in Porlock Avenue, South Harrow, as RT744 heads for Heathrow Airport in June 1978, a few weeks before the conversion of route 140 to Routemaster operation. The RT has managed to escape the attention of the souvenir hunters seeking LT radiator badges. The famous triangle was the hallmark of AEC buses for four decades, featuring on LT's vehicles from the STs and LTs of 1929 through to the Routemaster. Indeed, AEC, the abbreviation for the Associated Equipment Co, was originally a subsidiary of the LGOC and, even after its separation following the setting up of LT in 1933, continued to supply the majority of LT's chassis, except during the war years. It was as a result of AEC's virtual monopoly that only a small proportion of Leylands or other builders' buses were purchased by LT. Ironically, AEC was ultimately taken over by Leyland which then phased out the AEC marque and, in 1979, closed down the famous factory at Southall.

Room at the Top

Right: While on the subject of radiator badges, here is one which bears the National Bus Company's logo. A gleaming, but rather empty, RT3461 passes through Sanderstead in June 1977 on its way from Chelsham to West Croydon. Four London Country RTs were refurbished in 1977 in a desperate bid to overcome vehicle shortages, and three of the buses so treated received NBC livery. Unfortunately, RT3461's renaissance lasted only four months, whereupon it was no longer required for passenger service and was relegated to training duties.

California Here I Come

Left: RLH60 was one of the 76-strong lowbridge fleet built between 1950 and 1952 with Weymann 53-seat bodies. Harrow Weald garage had an allocation for route 230 due to a railway bridge in Headstone Lane which had a headroom of only 13ft 9in — RTs required a clearance of 14ft 6in. Large capacity one-person operated single-deckers took over on 14 June 1969, resulting in RLH60 exchanging the suburban setting of Northwick Park station, where it is seen here, for the warmer and sunnier climes of Long Beach, California.

Well Turned Out

Right: For a bus that is almost 10 years old, RF605 looks in remarkable condition as it stands at Addlestone garage on 2 August 1962. Like all the Country Area bus RFs, it has been converted to one-person operation and is able to operate as such, unlike its red counterparts which had to wait nearly six years after conversion before they could be used for OPO.
Geoff Rixon

Redundant and Re-employed

Below right: A contraction in rural services and the introduction of newer buses rendered many RFs surplus in the late 1960s, including RF605. This vehicle was one of several purchased by Halls of Hounslow and painted in their attractive Silverline livery for use as a transfer bus between terminals at Heathrow. Ten years on from Addlestone, RF605 stands outside Terminal Two. The vehicle behind is MLL740, BEA's last 1½-deck 'RF', which for six years worked alongside the fleet of Routemasters and luggage trailers carrying passengers to and from the West London Air Terminal at Gloucester Road.

First Day Cover
RM1200, in original condition complete with offside route number display, contributes to this busy lunchtime scene at Surbiton on 9 May 1962, the day after the last trolleybuses were withdrawn. *Geoff Rixon*

Hats off to the Trolleybus

Prince Albert pays his respects to London's last trolleybus, Class L3 No 1521 (a vehicle now happily preserved). Its place in history, however, could not be foreseen on this deserted Sunday morning — 7 August 1961 — at Holborn Circus. But the withdrawal of the north London routes and the unexpected decision of the Spanish to buy the entire fleet of postwar trolleybuses had seen the 'L3s' of 1939/40 vintage transferred to Fulwell and Isleworth depots and No 1521 was selected, along with No 1 (the 'Diddler'), for the final commemorative run on 8 May 1962. Despite this being a school day, I was determined not to miss the event and succeeded in persuading my mother to have me excused lessons for the afternoon on the pretext of a dental appointment. *R. C. Riley*

Past Over

Above: Evidence of roofboard mountings indicate that RF96 was once a Green Line coach, but it escaped modernisation in the mid-1960s and was demoted to bus work. It is seen here at West Croydon in June 1972 with patched-up Routemaster RML2316 for company. *Dave Edwards*

Stranger in the Camp

Right: An ex-Southampton Corporation Guy Arab looks out of place among the Routemasters in Godstone garage on 25 September 1971. RCLs Nos 2237 and 2250 maintain the traditional clean-cut Green Line coach image with no advertising. The 709 was the last crewed Green Line route, lasting until the Routemasters were replaced in May 1976. *R. C. Riley*

Unfrozen STL

Left: 'Unfrozen' was a term which completely mystified me as a child when, in 1958, I travelled from Ealing to Poplar trolleybus depot (much to my parents' horror when they found out!) to see the 11 'unfrozen' STLs stored there for possible conversion into lorries (conversions which never happened). These were the last STLs to remain in LT ownership and were part of a batch of 34 which were all withdrawn from passenger service by November 1952. The chassis were unfinished and 'frozen' when wartime bus building restrictions were introduced but in 1941 the ban was lifted to enable them to be completed. Eighteen examples, including STL2652 seen here at Purley in post-1946 Country livery, carried second-hand bodies and all the 'unfrozen' vehicles were distinguishable from other STLs by their unmatching front mudguards and louvred bonnets. STL2652 was withdrawn in May 1950 after only 8½ years' service. *C. Carter*

Provincial Leyland

Above: In late 1946 a total of 65 Leyland Titans of distinctly non-London appearance entered service and were tagged on to the prewar STD class. Falling foul of LT's standardisation policy, they were sold after only eight years' service, many going to Yugoslavia. STD165 was photographed at Buckhurst Hill, operating from Loughton garage. *C. Carter*

67

Misty Morning
Above: RT3840 crosses Blackheath on 15 November 1976. *Jim Collins*

Off the Beaten Track
Right: RF465 reposes among the autumn leaves at Old Lodge Lane, Purley, on 16 November 1976. *Jim Collins*

Name Dropper

Above: Two years after the demise of London Country's Guys (the GS type) in 1972, a successor from the same bodybuilder — ECW — appeared in the shape of short, narrow Bristol LHs (classified BN). With its name badge missing from below the radiator grille, BN51 stands at Welwyn North station on 28 September 1977. *Bill Ballard Collection*

Body Snatcher

Right: Following LT's decision to commence withdrawal of buses of the RT family by phasing out the Leylands first, a number of RTLs acquired obsolete roofbox RT-type bodies. RTL1456 tries to obliterate March Arch in August 1965. *Geoff Rixon*

Snow Progress

Above: Against the white landscape of Hainault Forest, RT2671 plods up Romford Road where, four months later, as part of a seven-vehicle cavalcade to commemorate the passing of the RT, it suffered the indignity of having to be pushed to the top of the hill by its passengers. After the conversion of route 87 in October 1978 (apart from one Saturday working), RTs were confined to the 62, which required 10 vehicles. A six-month reprieve due to a narrow bridge at Chadwell Heath enabled the RT class to reach its 40th year in LT service.

Leader of the Pack

Right: Mobile Instruction Unit 1037J stands derelict in West Ham garage on 24 September 1978. Who could possibly have imagined that a little over six months later, on 7 April 1979, this wreck would proudly stand at the head of the cavalcade marking the last run of the RT? Yet this is the unique body of RT1, complete with aluminium horizontal bands — a bus which took the transport world by storm in April 1939. The body sat on no less than four different chassis (not at the same time!), the underframes belonging to ST1140, RT19, STL2551/SRT45/1019J and finally RT1420, a Craven RT which had an altercation

with a low bridge in 1955. RT1 probably owes its longevity to the fact that it had a metal-framed body whereas the remainder of the prewar RT class had wooden-framed bodies which tended to sag with age. Nevertheless, because RT1's nether regions were not authentic LT declined to retain and restore this historic vehicle. So it went into private hands but, after the euphoria of its début in the cavalcade had died down, RT1 was back in trouble, heading for the USA and an uncertain future. Fears that it might become a burger bar prompted a repatriation campaign and the vehicle is now thankfully back in Britain in safe hands.
Geoff Rixon

Airmiss

Above: RT611 comes tantalisingly close to Heathrow Airport while working the twice-weekly route 444 linking Stanwell Moor with Staines. This route was introduced in March 1965 following the closure of the West Drayton to Staines West train service. During the late 1960s, I was a member of the BAA's Passenger Transport Panel and tried unsuccessfully to convince LT (Country Area) to run a service from Staines to Heathrow via the Cargo Tunnel, possibly by extending the 444 (and increasing its frequency!). The purpose was ostensibly to improve the lot of airport staff living in the Staines area by providing a direct bus service but I must confess that the possibility of green RTs mingling with their red brothers at Heathrow Central was an added incentive. Alas, it was not to be!

Waiting at the Church

Right: The external differences between the standard RF of 1951 and the modernised version of the mid-1960s are evident in this view at Dunstable in the summer of 1969. Green Line coach RF194 rests before commencing its long trek to Dorking, via Victoria, on route 712 while its Country bus companion, RF545, contemplates a more leisurely trip to Colney Heath on route 342. *C. Carter*

Pair of Trainers

So serious was the shortage of training vehicles in 1978 due to transfers to the depleted passenger fleet that LT did not wait to repaint some of the Routemasters repurchased from London Country, preferring just to apply the white bullseye and put the buses to work immediately. Exiting from the famous and now-defunct Chiswick Works is former Green Line coach RMC1516, followed by privately-preserved RT191, one of several veterans which LT was only too glad to hire for driving instruction.

On Broadway

Left: Childhood memories are evoked by this view of the New Broadway, Ealing, which once echoed to the sound of the wires as the 607 trolleybuses swept through on their journey from Shepherd's Bush to Uxbridge. Come to think of it, they only swept through on Sundays; most of the time they were crawling through in convoys of three or four! I hated cycling along the Uxbridge Road because, being silent, the trolleybuses would creep up behind unexpectedly, as you approached a bus stop, towering over your rear mudguard. The only warning was the telltale swish of the wires, but that could be from one coming towards you. RTs were also a familiar sight in Ealing, although route 274, worked

here by RT2520, was a late arrival, being introduced in November 1968. This service replaced a section of route 55 at its western end and also ran over part of my local route, the 97. I confess to remembering the RTs arriving on the 97, including a batch of green ones in 1953 which ran for three months and replaced my favourite STLs. The 274 kept the RT flag flying in Ealing until 1 October 1977, a few weeks after this photograph was taken.

Rescue Squad

Above: It's the last days of London's trolleybuses and No 1473, on the right, has disgraced itself at the Hampton Court terminus of route 604. Its front grille has been removed, a fitter is inside the vehicle and through the RT's windscreen Fulwell depot's Leyland Cub breakdown tender is visible. How prewar RT132 comes to be sandwiched between the trolleybuses is a mystery. Trolleybus No 1380 is also worth a mention because it was unique in carrying an 'FXF' registration. As for the route itself, the 604 started life as London United Tramways' trolleybus route 4 on 2 September 1931 and was renumbered in the LT series in 1935, vanishing when the Routemasters arrived on 9 May 1962. *Geoff Rixon*

End of Eastenders

Above: The replacement of RF-operated route 208A in 1959 by a new route 178 worked by RLHs brought these suburban and Country Area low-deckers into the East End. This was as close as they ever got to central London. RLH 61 had the honour of being LT's last lowbridge bus in service when it took its final duty on route 178 on 16 April 1971. Here it stands at Dalston garage along with RF400 and RLH54, the latter still carrying the old cream central relief band. *Julian Bowden Collection*

Lonely Vigil

Right: No wreaths or buntings, nor well-wishers (apart from me) to herald the departure of the last 97 bus. Saunders-bodied RT3068 stands forlornly in the rain at the Windmill Road (Greenford Red Lion) terminus on 29 November 1968. The RTs were replaced the next day by one-person operated single-deckers on route E2.

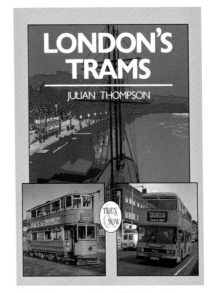
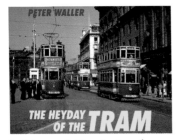
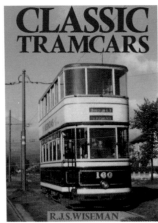